SOUL TALK

How to Have the Most Important Conversation of All

Kirk Byron Jones

Also By Kirk Byron Jones

Rest in the Storm: Self-Care Strategies for Clergy and Other Caregivers

Addicted to Hurry: Spiritual Strategies for Slowing Down

The Jazz of Preaching: How to Preach with Great Freedom and Joy

Morning B.R.E.W.: A Divine Power Drink for Your Soul

The Morning B.R.E.W. Journal

Holy Play: The Joyful Adventure of Unleashing Your Divine Purpose

Say Yes to Grace: How to Burn Bright Without Burning Out

The Sacred Seven: How to Create, Manage, and Sustain a Fulfilling Life

Say Yes to Grace: The Facebook Page Reflections

A Love Letter from God

Fulfilled: Living and Leading with Unusual Wisdom, Peace, and Joy

Refilled: Meditations for Leading with Wisdom, Peace, and Joy

Grace Sparks: Short Reflections to Encourage, Enlighten, and Energize Your Spirit

Calling Forth New Life: Becoming Your Freshest, Finest, and Fullest Self

Calling Forth New Life: The In-Visioning Journal

Just Because You're in a Storm Doesn't Mean the Storm has to be in You

Yes to Grace: Short Inspirations to Refresh Your Soul, Book One

To the Free and Enchanted Flight
of Souls Everywhere

Book Cover Design Credit: Sooraj Mathew
Email: aamijo2@gmail.com

Table of Contents

"You lead me beside still waters, You restore my soul."

—Psalm 23

"There is something that waits and listens for the sound of the genuine in yourself. It is the only true guide you will ever have. And if you cannot hear it, you will all of your life spend your days on the ends of strings that somebody else pulls."

—Howard Thurman

"Only by attending constantly to the inner voice can you be converted to a new life of freedom and joy."

—Henri J. M. Nouwen

"Listen to yourself and in that quietude you might hear the voice of God."

—Maya Angelou

Introduction

Allow Me to Present Your Soul

Though your soul may be more mystery to you than familiar reality, you are not a stranger to soul moments. When you smile for no reason, know something for sure without having learned it, or feel peace amid broken pieces, your soul is manifesting itself. Your soul is your hidden reservoir of limitless wisdom, peace, and joy. Your best guide for setting priorities and living at a sustainable pace is your soul. Your soul is the part of you God held last just before releasing your free flight into the world.

Your soul's home disposition is one of peaceful enthusiasm. Your soul's holy inclination is toward inciting high aspirations, but always from a place of deep contentment. Your soul wants to insure that your drive to succeed never runs roughshod over your peace, steadfastly insisting that your serenity be as deep as your ambition is high. Your soul knows and wants you to know that your best offering to the wider world derives from a place of inner peace.

Your soul has a knack for teasing and taunting you with new spaces of possibility in your relationships, vocational pursuits, and, most importantly, your being your freshest, finest, and fullest self in the world.

Your soul smiles as it assists you in cultivating a tenacious curiosity for the new, different, and challenging, for therein lies the impulse for you to explore the divine expanse, within and without, too big for words. Your soul wants you to ponder about the undiscovered terrains you sense but do not yet see. Your soul wants you to know the thrill of a certain kind of wondering that is as fulfilling as knowing. Your soul smiles whenever you are enchanted by mystery.

Your soul is the God-most part of you that has never known and will never know fear. Your soul is God's everlasting laughter in you. Your soul is God's Spirit in your spirit, filled to overflowing with lavish love, grace, and outrageous joy. More than anything else, your soul wants you to know how much you are madly adored by God in the grand hope that you will live *from* acceptance and not *for* acceptance.

Your soul loves you and will never ever lead you astray. This being true, your soul knows too much magnificent truth to be ignored, and is too utterly precious to be denied. I offer *Soul Talk* to you to help you get to know, understand, and value your Sacred Splendor better. You have heard everyone else out; now it is time to listen to your soul. Indeed, your conversation with your soul is the most important conversation of all.

In her wise and beautiful book, *Einstein and the Rabbi: Searching for the Soul*, Rabbi Naomi Levy concludes:

> *Your soul wants to teach you about your strength. It wants you to believe in your abilities and your gifts.*

It wants you to lift up your head with pride and claim your birthright: the life that is yours to experience. Your soul wants you to follow it through times of darkness, through the fog and confusion. Your soul will lead you to heights and to loves and to kindness.

Notable Features of Soul Speech

How do you know when your soul is speaking through your inner voice, and through spiritual nudges, feelings, and sightings? Soul communication comes forth from inside you, and from outside you, through persons, situations, and nature. There are certain primary features of soul speech that stand out for me. Your experience may result in highlighting additional primary qualities.

Distinct

The voice of your soul has its own unique sound. It comes from a place that is of this world, and yet beyond it at the same time. It is a voice that is gentle, but always strongly certain. Though soul voice may remind you of certain persons in your life, especially those with whom you have a special bond, the soul voice will always hold something strangely more in its sound.

Non-Anxious

Even when the message is serious and urgent, your soul will never communicate to create destructive tension within you, though it will, at times, risk planting seeds of creative tension. The soul sound is filled with peaceful reassurance. Soul voice is calm, always seeming to take your emotional state into deepest consideration. Your soul will never say anything to you that it believes you are truly unable to hear.

Clarity

Though we may muddle the soul's messages with our subsequent fears and doubts, initial soul message-sending is as clear as can be. Soul clarity is rooted in soul certainty. Never unsure about what it says, soul expression is direct and forthright.

Though we may be doubtful about what we hear, the soul is never doubtful about what it says.

Now there is this: Sometimes the soul's clarity is purposefully foggy. My experience is that the soul is intentionally unclear in order to create in you a desire to search further and dig deeper. The soul is not above using mystery to make you curious. Thomas Merton wrote, "Some things are too clear to be understood." Your not fully understanding is nothing to be ashamed of. Searches prompted by the soul telling some and keeping some can lead to some of the greatest discoveries of all.

Lighthearted

There is a space in your soul that has never known fear, and never will. Your soul knows that through it all, all is well. With such blessed assurance, the soul, more than it is known for doing, delightfully risks playfulness and joy. Your soul does not shy away from alluring you with prodding, nudges, and messages offered in hopes that you can't resist imagining, smiling, and laughing.

Challenging

As lighthearted as it can be, your soul will dare to ask questions designed to grow you. That being the case, the soul will utter things you may not want to hear, but need to hear in order to become better. Because the soul has your transformation in mind, it is more than willing to present truth that may first trouble you on the way to setting you free.

Patient

Nowhere is the soul's patience more evident than in its abiding willingness to repeat itself over and over again. With lavish grace, your soul will never make you feel guilty for not having heard something well the first, fourteenth, or fortieth time. Embedded within such patience is a relentless insistence that should not be underestimated or ignored.

The soul knows how ignorant we can innocently be, and sometimes deliberately choose to be. So the soul will keep seeking to arouse us with the same wisdom presented in different ways that we may eventually see the light.

Yet, soul tenacity is not beyond wounding. It is possible for soul patience to be strained. When this happens, our souls become restless. Feeling denied and diminished, your soul may cry out. Just because your soul is patient and persevering, doesn't mean it can't know deep suffering and rage. When your soul cries out, it is time to listen like never before.

Divine

There are those who believe that the voice of the soul and the voice of God are one. I will leave this for you to decide. I can say from my own experience of my soul offering some of the most compelling expressions of love, grace, and mercy I have known, that soul and God often speak as one. The soul will never offer you wisdom un-authorized by God. That it is divine also explains why the soul is so self-assured and non-defensive. It has nothing to prove; its presence is relaxed peaceful confidence. The soul's proximity to God is evi-denced by the peace of God it exudes.

Connection, Clarity, and Peaceful Confidence

Early in her writing career, esteemed author, Alice Walker, was told that she had to make major revisions to an article before it could be published. "You have to do this," explained the publisher. Walker re-sponded, "The only thing I have to do is save my soul." This was an instance of courageous soul-speak on behalf of itself.

Walker's experience points to three essential benefits of being in touch with your soul: 1. Divine Connection. 2. Clarity of Vision. 3. Peaceful Confidence.

Your soul connects you to your Source. Remembering and re-claiming your divinity is your greatest way to bless yourself. Sacred rootedness inspires clearer vision about who you really are and what you really want. A sense of God-ness and sureness of direction gives rise to confident peace empowering us to stand up and stand out.

Walker's connection, clarity, and peaceful confidence helped her to fend off being willfully ignorant of dehumanizing charades surrounding her, specifically: the lie that creative integrity needed to be compromised to achieve success. It is easy to be taken in and undone by limiting thoughts and perspectives that diminish us. Heeding the calls of the soul cultivating connection, clarity, and confidence within, insures that we will be loyal to that which is highest and royal inside of us.

Perennial Calls of Every Human Soul

While each of us will develop our unique way of relating with our soul, and hear many messages along the way, I believe there are three matters that every soul raises over and over again: *Authenticity*, *Freedom*, and *Transformation*. Authenticity is about you exploring and enjoying being who you deeply are. Freedom has to do with you living in the world as openly and nimbly as possible while maintaining a partnership with the dynamic flow of life. When we are one with life's flow, we have a comparable appreciation for both security and surprise. Transformation is inhabiting and expanding your growing edges as a way of life. In the words of the Jazz composer and pianist Edward "Duke" Ellington, our best offering is always "the next one." John O'Donohue writes ever so beautifully in *Anam Cara: Spiritual Wisdom from the Celtic World*:

> *The human heart is never completely born. It is being birthed in every experience of your life. Everything*

*that happens to you has the potential to deepen you.
It brings to birth within you new territories of the
heart.*

Being deeply who we are, in lighthearted relationship with the creative and challenging ebbs and flows of life, ever open and receptive to changes that grow us, brings overflowing joy to the soul.

Your soul will never say anything to diminish your commitments to personal authenticity, freedom, and transformation. On the contrary, it will find multiple ways to fan the fire under such sacred flames, allowing your light to shine and inspire for all the universe to see and celebrate. I have come to see personal authenticity, freedom, and transformation mattering most of all, above anything I can ever produce or acquire. My soul's witness along these lines is always beautiful liberating wisdom.

Unsung Gifts of Soul Talk

Alongside the deep peace, wisdom, and joy generated by soul talk are some fabulous unsung gifts:

Sensitivity to the Sacred

Patient attention cultivated in frequent soul talk helps you notice and appreciate the witness of the Spirit evident all the time. For example, many of us share the experience of feeling unusually blessed by a stranger's glance. Amid a throng of people, a lone smile in the distance can warm your heart. A blessing need not be directed toward us to be caught by us. Observing children at play can make your soul smile. Listening to someone's gentle tones with another can soften your heart. We are surrounded by small brilliant witnesses of glory. Attending to your soul's glory equips you to catch the rest of the glory all around us all the time.

Soul Friendship

Resist believing that your soulful conversation is just for you. Your ongoing deepening dialogue with yourself about what matters most readies you for conversations with others about what matters most. Your soul talk practice will deepen and enhance your dialogue with others. Personal soulful conversation increases your capacity to have genuinely soulful relationships. Such relationships should not be overlooked. In *Edge of Wonder*, Victoria Erikson offers:

> *Some people open up new worlds within us. Don't always assume there will be many more to come, as a great understanding between two beings is often rare.*
>
> *Be sure to nurture and fiercely appreciate these beautiful friendships and connections. You already know who they are.*

A soul friendship is one in which you are invited to share deepest wanderings and longings. It is characterized by the purest honesty, sharing, and reverence. A soul friend, more than anyone else, as said to me once, "holds that which is tender and sacred in you in holy embrace."

Soul friendships are impossible without an abiding commitment to one's own soul awareness and honesty. Without such, we are simply not outfitted to engage, embrace, and encourage others in the deep places. Having the courage to know yourself fully inspires and empowers you to know others fully.

Peace Overflow

A guest speaker was once accorded the following expression of gratitude:

Thank you for embodying a deep peace that brings out the depths in others and gives them permission to be fully themselves and to shine. What a blessing.

Inner peace is usually thought of in terms of benefiting the bearer of such splendid serenity. Yet inner peace has significant social potency. Think of those persons you know who exhibit a sustained calmness. They are not oblivious to it all; they just seem to have a rootedness about them enabling them to bear it all without breaking.

The soul is your reservoir of deep peace. The more you are at home with your soul, the more you are at home with your deep peace. Bearers of deep peace bestow peace without their even being aware of it. And not only peace, but wisdom, freedom, and grace for persons to be who they are without fear. Soulful peace offers invisible yet undeniable grace to others "to be fully themselves and to shine."

Justifying Soul Talk Time

How do you justify devoting time alone in an activity that does not immediately involve serving others, focusing on something that is not instantly measurable in terms of our cultural deities: acquisition and production? Spending time in the slow soft spaces of soul talk will challenge our addictions to speed, stimulation, and busyness. The worthiness of soul talk is precisely in its offering what we remain hungry for, in spite of our feasting on hurried and overloaded living: *deeper meaning in life.*

In recent years, I have developed a deeper appreciation for children's books. I try to read several of them each month. Such secret treasures are often dripping with insight, offering words and images pulling you into an experience that can remain with you long after the reading is over. Beatrice Alemagna's children's book, *On A Magical Do-Nothing Day,* tells the story of a little girl who goes outside in the rain on a day that feels as boring as it is dreary. Things go from bad to worse when she accidentally drops her portable video game device in a pond. She laments:

Without my game, I had nothing to do.

The rain felt like rocks were hitting me

I was a small tree trapped outside in a hurricane.

But then something magical happens. She follows four snails down a path, coming upon a muddy place:

*I bent down and dug my fingers into the mud where
a thousand seeds and pellets, kernels, grains, roots,
and berries touched my fingers and hands. An underground world full of treasures that I could feel.*

Time with your soul will be like surveying an underground world full
of treasures that you never knew were there. Any justification that
you need for spending time alone and away investigating this world
will come from your discoveries, and their revolutionizing impact on
your more empowered and enchanted personhood going forward.

The 7 Soul Talk Steps

The method offered in *Soul Talk* for maintaining a continual dialogue
with your soul includes the following seven steps:

1. Be Still.
2. Lay Burdens Down.
3. Listen Deeply.
4. Don't Run Away.
5. Be Honest.
6. Be Gentle.
7. Welcome New Truth.

My soul talk moments are usually early in the morning, and are about
5 to 20 minutes long. The steps I share with you, based on my own

soul talk experience, need not occur in chronological order. For example, it is not uncommon for me to hear a new truth first, choose to not run away, and instead move to a place of stillness to continue listening deeply in the stillness. This example is just the reverse of the steps as presented. While I render the steps in a certain order, that order is not etched in stone. Be free to engage your soul in the way that seems most natural for you. Use my steps as a guide. Look to manifest their expression in the way that seems most genuine to you at the time. You may across time develop a preferred sequence of steps, even choosing to add or to subtract from the ones I offer. The point of it all is to make soul talk a vital part of your everyday life in one way or another.

Showing Your Soul to Yourself: Chronicling Your Soul Talk

I have journaled since leaving my first pastorate in 1984. Founding and leading Beacon Light Baptist Church in my home of New Orleans, LA was so exciting and fulfilling that I wanted to make sure I remembered as much of it as possible. My journaling practice expanded over the years, as I began to appreciate how much it helped to keep me awake to my life. More than helping me to stay in the know about my life, journaling helps me to stay in charge of my life. Deliberately recording experiences and explorations that matter makes me more deliberate about not just responding to life, but intentionally and thoughtfully creating life. I now maintain several journals, one exclusively devoted to my soul talk dialogue. Journaling helps me to show my soul to myself.

Whether you choose to use the accompanying *Soul Talk Journal* or not, I strongly encourage you to take some moments to record highlights from your soul talk sessions. My habit is to jot a word or phrase during the session itself. Often but not always, I then take a moment to summarize any messages, images, ideas, and impressions that may have surfaced during the session. Doing so helps me to stay alert for recurring themes. It is important for me to note guidance that I am led to put into practice in some way.

Tracking inner dialogue sessions also increases my confidence in soul talk as I observe specific instances in which it made a difference.

As you journal, here are three tips for you to consider. First, experiment writing with your non-dominate hand. Most of us have less control over our non-dominate hand when writing. This can lead to writing that is not over-thought and less contrived. Using your non-dominate hand may make it easier for you to unlock the hidden wisdom of your soul. Second, pay careful attention to writing that surprises you in some way. Notice what seems to be written more *through* you than *by* you. Ponder what you write, but had not intended to. These words may offer to you what the beloved Howard Thurman referred to as "the growing edge." Third, don't just write, doodle. Let yourself sketch images as well as write words. Sometimes the soul can effectively say in an image, what you may need hundreds of words to accurately express.

Journaling your soul talk conversations helps you to keep such vital dialogue as a priority in your life. For Anne Morrow Lindbergh, chronicling living enlivened living:

> *I must write it all out at any cost. Writing is thinking. It is more than living, for me it is conscious living.*

Perhaps journaling will become for you what it has become for me and so many others: *A soul-growth necessity.*

Have Fun!

In the movie *Patch Adams,* a young unorthodox physician in training is almost dismissed from medical school for displaying "excessive happiness." In the the movie *The Color Purple*, Sophia laments, "I know what it feels like to want to sing and have it beaten out of you." Both Patch Adams and Sophia are opposed by the enemies of delight. Your soul never was or ever will be counted among the enemies of delight.

Your soul is aware of the pitfall of being so focused on order and tradition that we fail to appreciate God's appetite for divine lunacy and sacred surprise.

Your soul talks should not be heavy hearted affairs. Though there will be times of engaging deep brokenness, the natural inclination of the soul is toward joyful lightheartedness. So don't be afraid to laugh and smile with your soul. Don't be shocked by surprising questions, whimsical answers, and the soul seeming silly at times. To live with soul is to hear the rhythms of new possibilities and not be afraid to *play* along.

Finally, you will find poetry at the end of each chapter. I hope these brief entries are as much blessing to you as the prose contained here. Poetry has a way of opening me up and expanding me in ways prose does not. I hope the same for you, and for your soul to say things to you in the spaciousness surrounding the poetry that I have not said in this book, that your soul wants you to hear.

Soul Glee

There is

a deep

soul glee

that does

not make

a sound

lest it

start laughing

and never stop.

Soul Wish

More than

anything else,

your soul

wishes you

fierce freedom

for exploration

and enchantment.

All Yearning Lost

Once when I went within

seeking for what my soul wanted,

I found plush grass

and fell upon all yearning lost.

And my soul said, "That."

Soul Settle Down

Settle down

in your soul

to restore

your peace,

regulate

your pace,

and reset

your priorities.

1

Be Still

"Be still, and know that I am God!" Psalm 46:10

The Diva, Stillness, and You

If the word diva means bold, beautiful, and in charge, Theoclecia Bijou, my high school vocal music teacher was the first one that crossed my path. Always immaculately dressed and adorned, she had this charmed, playful, but also no-nonsense way about her. I remember so well her manner of putting you in your place if you tried to hold a conversation with someone while she was instructing. She simply stopped talking, looked at you, and said, "I'll wait until you're finished." Or, if she was feeling particularly grand on that day, "What you have to say is obviously more important than what I am being paid to say, so class, let's all listen in."

Theoclecia Bijou was not one to compete for your undivided attention. You gave it or you didn't. If for some reason you were compromised in rendering it, she would simply wait on you. Your soul is like my beloved music teacher in this way. Your soul will not compete with other voices in order to be heard. Your soul will wait patiently for you to choose to offer the attention of your silence and stillness.

Listening for the Sound of the Genuine

"There is something that waits and listens for the sound of the genuine in yourself. It is the only true guide you will ever have. And if you cannot hear it, you will all of your life spend your days on the ends of strings that somebody else pulls."

These words from Howard Thurman are among the words I cherish most. In full disclosure, without these words echoing in my mind and spirit, I may never have written this book. I wrote this book out of a deep desire to help others access "the sound of the genuine." I once wrote the following words in one of my personal journals:

How do I help myself "listen to the sound of the genuine" more? How do I help others to do it. In a flash, I sense that it has something to do with allowing ourselves to be vulnerable to our deepest thoughts, fears, and feelings. Being totally open to all that we are, our known and unknown. If we can relax into the totality of our being, all our sides can have their say without fear of being castigated. In this free zone of free expression, our sound of the genuine may be detected, cultivated, and trusted more and more.

Stillness is that free zone of free expression.

Stillness May Be Easier Than You Think

You may have the impression that stillness is harder to practice than it really is. You need not become a master of contemplation or meditation to become adept at practicing small periods of mental ease and relaxation. Two important keys at doing so are wanting to and taking the time to. If you are new to stillness-making, start off with relaxing your mind for just 10 seconds. Slowly increase your time length to a minute then to several minutes. Do so each day, perhaps several times a day.

Here are some proven stillness helps:

- Slow your breathing and take deeper breaths.
- Focus on empty items, such as an empty vase to help you feel empty.
- Observe a burning candle.
- Listen to soothing music.
- Resist thinking about anything at all.
- Behold without judging.
- Image still water and relax your soul there.
- Focus on a picture of serenity.
- Repeat a comforting scripture.
- Listen to the sounds of nature.

The goal with your stillness practice is to reach a space of what poet Mary Oliver refers to as "not-thinking, not-remembering, and not-wanting." It may be difficult at first. Thoughts will prove contrary and want to disrupt your stillness moment. Gently wave them on and refocus your attention on the fullness of emptiness.

Stillness Tears

One morning not long ago, I found myself in the throws of unexpected crying during a moment of stillness. I have learned not to resist such tears and to let them fall. I realized they were linked to an experience shared with a friend the day before, at a restaurant where music could be heard in the background. Amid our delightful dialogue, I suddenly heard the unmistakable trumpet sound of Louis Armstrong, followed by his gloriously growling singing. I stopped midstream in our conversation, causing my friend to do the same. I savored the glorious Jazz offering and said, "There must be a God because there is that horn and there is that voice." My friend smiled in sacred agreement. Remembering and reliving a moment of soulful bliss made me cry tears of appreciation.

Resist resisting your stillness tears. Your tears are necessary for hallowing tender moments, and for health and healing. Much of what is ailing many of us may be linked to wounds barely noticed and tears never shed. Stillness allows us to drop our resistance, giving our tears a chance to fall from sadness, gladness, and everything in between.

Letting Nothingness Have Its Way

"By falling silent and listening, we hear a deeper speech, that of the divine."

—*Gregg Levoy*

I have become a student of my first mood of the day. Often that mood is up-beat and anticipatory of the new day's explorations and experiences. Then again there are days of feeling weighted down by this or that that I can name, or something that remains a mystery to me. So many days are somewhere in between these two poles. And there is another mood. This mood has me feeling nothing at all. It often follows a day of extreme engagement and energy release. This mood is fed by an inner fatigue. Yet, in full disclosure, the nothingness is sometimes laced with doubts regarding the meaning of life: Is this all there is? What if what I hold to be precious and true is not all that precious and true at all?

The nothingness mood used to be the most troubling mood of all to me, but not anymore. I have come to embrace it as a release of sorts. A time to be free of all obligatory thoughts, preferences, and familiarities. The space of nothingness creates a clearing for me where I can rest for awhile, and when wanting to, mentally move about in new wide spaces of clearing and possibility.

I have discovered my soul talk time to be safe spaces for such wandering. My soul does not pressure me to think this or that, or to think at all. My soul lets me meander and loiter. My soul trusts me without my baggage, and, in fact, challenges me to travel more lightly during and apart from soul talk moments.

Nothingness need not be experienced as threatening or wasteful. Stripped of our dependencies, we can feel another way of being, more free and receptive before the unknown. And blessing galore, seduced by nothingness, we are more likely to not only engage nothing's mystery, but from time to time, kiss it.

The Hidden Movement of Stillness

I once attended a dance performance by the legendary Bill T. Jones. That night his non-movement was just as amazing as his movement. There were points in his performance when he held a pose for an extended period of time. We were on the edge of our seats waiting for him to move and not move. His stillness danced before our very eyes. There was as much vibrancy and vitality in his stillness as there was in his physical movement. I recall another iconic dancer, Judith Jamison, suggesting in her magnificent book, *Dancing Spirit*, that even when we are still, we are still moving as dynamic energy continues to emanate from our bodies. This is the marvelous hidden movement of stillness.

Due to its nature of silence and non-motion, stillness may be devalued in a culture fueled by noise and non-stop movement. We underestimate stillness to our detriment. Stillness is not passive. Stillness is an act of unsuspected and unusual spiritual strength. Stillness yields space to sense our vast inner wealth, harness vital energy for genuine transformation, and experience satisfying and empowering soul contentment. Stillness sensitizes us to the nudges and whispers of the Holy Spirit and our sacred inner wisdom. Ignited by such pure and sure creative inspiration, our being and doing is nothing short of dancing with God.

Morning BREW

Be Still.

Receive God's Love.

Embrace Yourself.

Welcome the Day.

What the Soul Loves

The soul loves

breath

freedom

space

and a whole lot of

take your time.

Soul Pleas

Breathe deeply

more often.

Slow down.

Lighten your load.

Make spaces.

Please.

Exquisite Peace

Take a moment
to feel the
exquisite peace
of still waters
within you.

Lounging in God's Grace

God,

help me

to be still,

to lounge

in Your grace

and listen

to Your song,

and to hear

my song

in Yours.

Post-it Note from Soul

Please remember

that your

deep peace

is inexhaustible,

and, not least of all,

portable.

Where Love Lives

If you can be

still enough

long enough

there is a place within

on the other side of silence

where love lives.

2

Lay Burdens Down

Surrendering Your Heavy Load

Believe it or not, one of my favorite hobbies is playing video games. I actually began playing with the Intellivision gaming systems way back when. I took a break, but returned to gaming after experiencing vocational burn-out and finding myself not being able to sufficiently answer a physician's simple question: *What do you do to relax?*

Now, I have several answers for that question, gaming being one of them. I especially enjoy role playing games in which your character is tasked with challenging adventures of exploration and discovery. With each successful engagement, you "level up" in experience and skill. A part of the thrill of such gaming is managing and viewing your character's growth in stature and strength.

In some role playing games, encumbrance can become a problem. Encumbrance occurs when a character is too weighted down by items picked up along the way to continue exploring. Normal speed is replaced with your character trudging along. The quickest way to fix encumbrance is to drop some of the items you are carrying. Choosing just what to drop, from armor, weapons, gems, and various other items, is the challenge in the challenge. But drop some things you must, if you are going to continue your journey at a reasonable pace.

As you engage your soul talk moments, it will not take long for you to discover encumbrance. When you seek to be silent, it is not uncommon for concerns and worries to surface and challenge the very stillness you seek. This challenge must be faced. You cannot engage the natural lightness of your soul with the weight of the world on your shoulders. You must trust surrendering your heavy load.

Imagining Being Burden-less

Though a formidable threat, encumbrance during soul talks is not insurmountable. To lay your burdens down, see yourself doing so in your imagination. As you encounter worries and concerns in stillness, greet them by name, and gently excuse them from your consciousness. Choose to stop thinking about them for the duration of your soul talk moment. This may not be easy at first. Initial attempts may even prove unsuccessful, but stay with it. Soon you will feel yourself leveling up in your power to momentarily cease bearing burdens.

Pay attention to mental images that work well for you in this regard. I find imagining myself beneath a waterfall very helpful in feeling burden-free. You may find drawing from your familiarity with Scripture to be most effective. Don't just read about being in God's presence beside still waters, see and feel yourself there. I remember, as a child listening to congregants sing in the African-American church tradition, "Take Your Burdens to the Lord and Leave Them There." There are times when I imagine myself doing just that to feel a sense of freedom from the weight of it all. Use and develop the gift of sacred imagination to lay your burdens down.

Some persons measure their spiritual maturity by how heavy their burdens are. Lightness of heart is a surer sign. You never know how heavy your load is until you find the courage to stop and let it go. Trust letting go of heavy loads, especially burdens you were not meant to carry in the first place.

An essential feature of the soul is its sacred lightness. Experiencing this lightness will be one of the most comforting and compelling aspects of your soul talk times. Learn to meet lightness with lightness, and your soul talks will take you to places of peace that you have never known before. Within such peace is wisdom and joy too good not to be true.

Letting Go of Thinking

When our youngest, Jovonna, was a little girl, she once asked why I looked so angry. It perplexed me because in that moment I was not angry at all. But I was in deep thought. She had interpreted my pondering for being troubled. Once I made the connection, I explained to her that I wasn't mad, I was "just thinking." Her response did not get me off the hook: "Why are you always thinking?"

At that time in my life, more often than not, I was thinking about family matters, church matters, school matters, cultural matters. Here a thought, there a thought, everywhere a thought thought. I had to learn how to not think all the time. I did and the impact has been life-changing.

One of the things that helped me learn to suspend thinking for a while was placing an empty bowl on my desk. Whenever I wanted to empty my mind of everything, if only for a few moments, I would focus on the non-contents of the bowl. The bowl's emptiness helped me to feel my own cessation of thoughts. It wasn't easy at first. But as suggested by many, I went easy on myself and on the thoughts that tried to intrude. I learned how to patiently hold them at bay until I was ready to entertain them. The more I experienced the soothing ease of not thinking, the more I was convinced I would benefit by having more of this less in my life.

Momentarily letting go of thinking completely is essential and possible for soul talk. The soul prefers undivided attention. Your soul will not compete with other voices. It will wait for the silence and stillness it respectfully insists on. Only when we present it with clear skies, will it present us with clear understandings sufficient enough to have us thinking things we have never thought before. Non-thinking opens the door to new thinking.

Laying Aside The Burden of Over-Achievement

I was a chronic over-achiever, and it almost cost me my life. My wake-up call came almost three decades ago when in the middle of preaching, I suddenly stopped. I could still speak; the problem was I did not have the energy to do so. I was so very tired. To that point,

I primarily lived my life through my goals and achievements. They were not bad in and of themselves. What was deadening was my over-fixation on the doing dimension of existence, and my under-valuation of life that has nothing whatsoever to do with striving and straining even for the most laudable of ends.

The liberating lesson that I learned in the aftermath of my abrupt sermonic halt, and one that I am still embracing more deeply, is that living is not just achieving. Living is more than achieving. When we see living as only achieving, we miss the manifold splendor of life that is grace. The adventure that is life is not just about earning and winning. The adventure includes more deliberately embracing what we can never claim responsibility for. The adventure is not just about grit; the adventure is about grace.

One of the most significant things you can lay aside when speaking with your soul is the need to meet any standard whatsoever. Your soul does not need to see your score card. Your soul only need see you, with appreciation for achievements, but not addicted to them. This is the only way to behold and benefit from the limitless dimension of life independent of our struggling and striving. This is life perceived as grace and favor, first and foremost.

An Invitation to Linger

I once shared with a friend about the reflective spaces I had been recently occupying. Her response to me was short and oh so powerful: "Linger, my friend, linger." When was the last time someone told you to linger? When was the last time you even heard or used the word? Ours is not a lingering culture. To linger, wait around with no specific agenda, smacks of irresponsibility and negligence. And yet, my friend's urging me to do so seemed so appealing and so right.

Our souls love it when we linger, when we stop pushing and pulling and allow ourselves to be at ease in body, mind, and spirit. Lingering allows for savoring, respite, and restoration. Lingering lets us listen to the deep spaces and places, enabling us to excavate even deeper spaces and places in ourselves. Lingering lets us feel the breeze of the spirit inviting us to let it be well with our souls. Enjoy just lingering.

Letting Yourself Feel Free

One morning, as I sat in a moment of silence and stillness, looking out my home office window, my eyes moistened. This is a sign to bring myself to alertness, and simply wait for thoughts to surface without strenuous effort on my part. When something did emerge that morning, I was led to write the following words:

In that moment
when water flows
for no reason,
perhaps it is
just your
feeling free
from that which
had you bound.

We grow so accustomed to living stressed, that feeling ease may seem foreign. What right have we to feel a deep and abiding peace, not just for an instant, but for extended moments in time? What right have we not to? Indeed, if we are to engage life with energy and creativity, we must become increasingly comfortable abiding with our inner reservoir of freeing peace. This is not a selfish indulgence. Letting yourself feel burden-less and unbound is a necessary action for living with replenished hope.

Soak Your Soul

Before shouldering

any burden

at all

this day,

soak your soul

in the waters

of God's grace.

Unnecessary Burdens

Watch what

you pick up.

Many burdens

are needlessly

self-imposed.

Be Rid of Resentment

Resist holding
resentment
for what others are
unable or unwilling
to see in you.
Bless yourself,
and journey on.

Glad Surrender

When you

give your all

and your all

doesn't seem

good enough,

give it all

to God.

Carry One Day

Carry one day.

Put yesterday down.

Don't pick up tomorrow.

Carry one day.

Prayer to Be at Ease With a Lighter Load

Dear God,

Free me

from the need

to feel

overly burdened.

Help me

to guiltlessly

get used

to living

with a lighter load.

Amen.

3

Listen Deeply

Turn Down the Noise

Noise-canceling devices are amazing. When I first used such a headset during a flight, I kept touching the on/off button. I had no idea that airplane engines were so loud. With the noise turned down, I could hear my self thinking better, not to mention my sweet Jazz sounds more clearly.

Listening to your soul is worth turning the noise down. Your soul not only deserves to be listened to, but listened to ferociously. To do so is to benefit from the soul's deep wisdom and to cultivate the capacity for soulful listening in every dimension of your life. When honored with listening, the soul rewards us with tantalizing longing for deeper listening and noticing to the world within and the world at large. Not only do we learn how to listen; we learn to love listening. Such Listening yields deep wisdom, and a capacity for listening to yourself, others, and our troubled, yet still terribly enchanted sacred world.

The Soft Voice of the Soul

Solitude and silence are so vital for soul talk because the soul often speaks softly. Why? I can think of four possible reasons. One reason may be that whether we feel it or not, there is a deep part of us that is always at peace. We all have some still water within us. The soul's soft voice may be related to its peacefulness, and secondly, to its certainty. A good deal of our raised volume derives from trying to be heard and sound sure. Soul existence does not hinge on our validation, nor soul surety on our confirmation. The soul's soft voice is its self-contained confidence in its deep truth.

Thirdly, the soul may speak softly for fear of frightening us with alarming truth. Finally there is this: Something said just above a whisper encourages more concentrated effort to pay attention. Your soul may speak low so you can listen high.

Courageous Listening: Hearing What We Don't Want to Hear

There is so much we would rather not hear: criticism, an upsetting revelation, tragic news, confirmation of failure and more. With the wonder of life comes the horror of life. We can turn a deaf ear to undesirable communication, but the result is missing too much vital growth on the backside of what we perceive to be bad news. A worthwhile alternative is to practice courageous listening: intentional and deliberate attention to sounds that threaten us. This will not be easy given that we are not fond of perceived assaults on our comfort, control, and overall sense of well-being.

Courageous listening, choosing to pay attention in spite of feeling threatened, can present us with data to grow we may have no other way of attaining. Genuine transformation hinges on our choosing to hear from a friend, a situation, or your soul, new possibilities buried in what initially sounds unbearable.

What actions build courageous listening? First, be more questioning than judgmental. We shut down transformation by immediately dismissing what we don't have to and don't want to hear. Be on alert for this tendency and pronounce an inquiry where you would render a ruling. Second, focus on listening with patience. Do this by allowing for pauses before responding. We rush what we would be rid of. Give unsettling communication a chance to be fully heard and comprehended. You may hear something surprisingly revealing and reviving. Third, listen to understand first. So much of our listening is really begrudged space observed before speaking. We tend not to listen to understand, but to bide our time before we can get a word it. What does it mean to focus as much effort on genuine understanding as getting in the next word, or the last word? Finally, root your worth in who you are not what you hear. We can more readily risk hearing what we don't want to hear if we remember that nothing we can ever hear has the power to ultimately separate us from God's grace, mercy, and love.

Practice courageous listening. There are expansive new vistas on the other side of hard truth.

Hearing and Honoring New Questions

A truly saved soul is an exploring and expanding soul, a soul set free for new challenges and questions. Yes, questions. New questions are unsung liberators. While answers can satisfy, they can also enslave. A challenging, if uncomfortable new question has the power to transform us for the better.

Get into the habit of bringing questions to soul talk sessions, and listening for questions raised during these precious moments of tender contemplation. In the safety of your interiority, you can risk asking within what you may be afraid to ask in the company of others. What you may never ask in a crowd is always eligible for inquiry during your soul talk. And you can trust these moments. Soul interrogations are never meant to diminish you, but always to lift you up, to help you embrace more freely and fully your innate divinity. To hear God is to practice tenacious openness.

Personal Soul Inquiries

What sorts of things might the soul surface as wondrous questions? Here are some of my own sacred unforgettable inquiries heard as I gave myself over to deep listening:

- *What if being saved involves not settling for living anything less than an enchanted life?*

- *Whatever led you to believe that life is supposed to be more burdensome trek than lighthearted journey?*

- *How much are you willing to lose to gain what you can hardly imagine?*

- *Why must change be more dread than dance?*

- *Don't you know that God is as much in the mud as God is in the rainbow. Why are you so afraid of getting dirty?*

- *What if exploration meant more to you than production and acquisition?*

- *Why aren't you focusing more time and energy on things that enchant you?*

- *What if you already have more than you ever wanted?*

- *Where do you wish to see new life? What are you willing to do to keep rising?*

Soul and Mystery

Said Soul,

"I will never tell you all I know;
I must share some and keep some
that you may always
behold the mystery
more satisfying than knowing."

The foregoing words fell into my spirit one morning after coming across the word mystery while reading. While I am not a huge fan of mysteries as a literary genre, the reality of mystery has always attracted me, especially in regard to spirituality. I find it necessary to cultivate a religious experience that leaves room for what I cannot presently perceive or understand. During Bible Study last evening, a congregant spoke of needing to leave "wiggle room" for God. Perhaps my needing mystery is my leaving wiggle room for God.

The natural God-ness of the soul necessitates that the soul hold and honor mystery. So we can expect the soul's knowingness to be shrouded in a not-knowing that may leave you wanting depending on your attitude toward mystery. Mystery need not be frustrating. On the contrary, mystery can enliven us with continued interest, desire, and curiosity. Moreover, I find mystery nurtures humility and spaciousness within me, leading me to a mindset of lavish openness and radical receptivity.

Before our deepest listening, the soul will never tell all it knows. It will tell some and keep some to honor the majesty of mystery. This is nothing to mourn. When reverenced, mystery is as satisfying as knowing. Mystery, with its sometimes unsettling ambivalence and ambiguity, offers a golden invitation to keep searching. Do so and you may discover the precious gem of continually refreshed curiosity. This is a treasure worth having.

Listening Deeply Leads to Seeing Deeply

William Claxton makes the following confession in Jazz Seen, his wonderful collection of jazz-related photographs:

> *I love the music. Always have. But I've always been fascinated by the way it's produced, as well, by the way it looks. By the body language and the movements of musicians as they play, by the way the light strikes their faces.... I guess you could say I listen with my eyes.*

When it comes to seeing, most of us are on automatic pilot. We don't think about it; we just look wherever our attention leads us, and usually not for long. Claxton raises the possibility of an alternative way of seeing: seeing with concentration. We know what it means to listen more intently, even if we don't do it often enough. Seeing more intently may be completely new territory. If Claxton's book is any clue, this new land of "listening with eyes" is well worth exploring.

As you become better at listening, seek to apply your new capacity to all of your other senses, especially seeing. Here is a prayer to support your process:

Dear God,

> *Help me not to just look,*
> *but to see and to see deeply,*
> *beyond preconceived expectations*
> *that obscure my best vision.*
> *Amen.*

Soul Searching Questions

The soul is not the only one who gets to ask the questions during soul talks, you do. Here are some questions to give voice to. Remember to give deep ear to your soul's responses:

What do you want me to know most of all right now?
What have you been repeating to me?
How can I listen to you better?

What do you perceive to be the biggest threat to our ongoing dialogue?
What is enhancing my life?

What is diminishing my life?
What am I missing seeing that's right before my eyes?
Among my friends, who can I trust most?
What do I need to remember?
What do I need to forget?

How do you try to get my attention?
When do you feel me ignoring you?
How am I resisting love?
Where should I turn for help?
What do you feel me fearing most of all?

What makes you angry?
What makes you smile?
What makes you want to dance?
What gives you peace?
Where are you leading me?

God's Fingerprints

Anything

that opens

the mind

or softens the heart

has God's fingerprints

all over it.

Accepting Acceptance

There is a love

not earned

and a joy

not won.

Upon acceptance,

your tears

will be

gift too.

Every Now and Then

Every now

and then,

your soul

will remind you

that you are

much larger

than you think.

Message from Loitering Moon

Loitering moon
in morning light said,
"Do not be afraid of
the lingering love of God."

Search Thirst

Sometimes

your soul

won't answer

you directly

in order

to create

a thirst

for search.

When Your Soul Goes Quiet

When your soul

goes silent,

trust that

the quiet

you hear

is a new pathway

being cleared

for faithful passage.

70

4

Don't Run Away

A Memorable Confession

I will never forget an email I received from a person after a workshop focused on overcoming addiction to hurry. A mother shared with me her struggle to seek silence and solitude. Her son had been murdered and she was still grieving. She said that her constant moving was necessary in order to avoid agonizing feelings of grief that surfaced whenever she kept still for long in one place. Her running was running away from hurt, suffering, and pain. How utterly human and understandable.

Yet, there is no getting around the fact that deeply enriching soul talk will necessitate our slowing down, and coming to a complete halt. This will be true especially when what surfaces during a soul talk session gives us reason to run. And yet, resisting running is essential to living an awake and transformed life. Anthony DeMello makes this strikingly clear in his provocative book, *Awareness*:

> *The chances that you will wake up are in direct proportion to the amount of truth you can take without running away. How much are you ready to take? How much of everything you've held dear are you ready to have shattered, without running away?*

What We Fear the Most Might Be What Sets Us Free

Susan Goldsmith Wooldridge includes the following testimony in her wonderful book, *Poemcrazy: Freeing Your Life With Words:*

> *My friend Mary Ann told me once about a lizard trapped in a room where she was house sitting. She couldn't rescue the lizard because it was afraid of her, so It died, hiding from its source of freedom. This made Mary Ann think that often what we fear the most might be what frees us.*

Pay special attention to realizations that you resist during your soul talks. Be an alert observer of your thoughts, feelings, and bodily sensations. Try to remain in any discomfort long enough to be more curious than uneasy. Then follow the footsteps of your curiosity. Eventually your being afraid will give way to being interested. Being interested in what frightens you is the key to embracing the true freedom on the other side of fear, that is always more than trading one cell for another. A truly saved soul is an exploring and expanding soul, a soul set free. Your free soul seeks to free you.

Facing Hard Truths

As I am completing this, the film *Black Panther* is taking the world by storm. The amazing cinematic offering is filled with many important lessons. One of the most significant lessons is the importance of facing disturbing truths that threaten cherished understandings and perceptions. Perhaps, the Black Panther's biggest struggle and victory in the movie is facing a hideous secret of his heritage, and forging beyond it to create new avenues of cooperation. The journey to and through hard truth is not without great strife, suffering, and loss.

Silence and stillness during your soul talk times set the stage for truths to surface that you normally are allowed to keep at bay with busyness. The challenge is to let these truths have there say. What we may not have considered consciously for some time may arise during a soul talk. Let it. Don't run away. Let the tears flow; resist the resistance to deeper listening. When you are able, take notes. Ask questions. The great unsung remedy for fear is curiosity. Learn to listen courageously.

If you need to and can, share your new awareness with a trusted friend. It may be a truth so difficult that professional assistance is needed. If so, acquire the professional help you need. One of the greatest blessings of being in touch with our souls is touching truths that, though troubling, have the capacity to set us free in extraordinary ways. Hard truth is one of the most liberating realities of all. But before it sets you free such truth may scare you death, and then, to new life.

May you not be counted in the "we" identified by W.H. Auden:

We would rather be ruined than changed. We would rather die in our dread than climb the cross of the moment and let our illusions die.

When Your Soul Cries Out

I have held on to a post card gifted to me by one of my dear former seminary students. The post card displays a stunning photograph of Billie Holiday taken in 1948 by William Paul Gottlieb, best known for his renderings of the leading performers of jazz in the 1930s and 40s. You can view the image on the cover of his book, *The Golden Age of Jazz.* The singer's head is thrown back to the left. Her eyes are closed and her mouth open wide. You can almost hear the sound of the image coming forth from the picture. It is a sound of pain, grief, hurt, and even rage. Billie Holiday is singing from her soul and her soul is crying out.

Though your soul's home space is a place of peace, that peace may be disturbed. It takes a great deal to disturb the pure peace of the soul, but when such a disruption occurs, the soul is capable of erupting. Should and when this happens, you must resist denying the soul's cry. You must not run away. When your soul cries out, listen. Listen like never before.

Sometimes, your soul will object to someone's attempts to continually diminish you. Respect your soul's objection. Davis Whyte is so tenderly right when he concludes his poem *Sweet Darkness* as follows:

…anything or anyone
that does not bring you alive
is too small for you.

The soul may also cry out against injustice, the wounding and slaughter of the innocent and unnamed grief. Moreover, the threat of an idol god will cause the soul to cry out. An idol god is anything we attribute ultimate status, to our own detriment and diminishment. Be alert to the soul's cry against such false deities. For example, I have felt my soul more than once wail against my insistent loyalty to the idols of busyness and hurry. Once, I heard my soul ask in sanctified rebellion, "Who made doing as much as you can as fast as you can God?" Adding, "Life does not need your exhaustion." My soul was helping me to identify and dethrone idol gods that meant me no good. My soul was doing its job. *exhaustion*

Barely Noticed Blessings

Chronic rushing diminishes life in so many ways. One truly unacceptable diminishment is our not taking the time to appreciate the blessings we are standing right smack in the middle of. Ever reaching for this and that at break-neck speed detracts from our savoring what we already have in hand. What if more intentional and deliberate savoring contributes to a deeper sense of satisfying well-being? Perhaps we would be less inclined to keep scratching and reaching for that which we already have. What blessings can you think of that you have barely noticed? What if you already have more than you ever wanted?

Don't Run Away from Peace

Your soul will cry out, and your soul will make you cry tears of sadness, and tears of purest joy. Regarding the latter, there will be moments when your soul will overwhelm you with perfect peace. And you will cry. You will cry because it will surprise you with how suddenly it will appear. You will cry because what sneaks up on you is all gift and all love. It is the feeling that all is well disconnected from any striving, pushing, or pulling on your part.

To feel such peace may be jarring at first, but resist the urge to flee. You can be so conditioned to earning whatever good comes your way, that receiving gracious peace can seem wrong in some way. And yet, grace is what God is always sending our way whether we like it or not. Perhaps the best goal of spiritual maturity is to learn to love grace. So when during a soul talk, you suddenly find yourself lost in the sweetest peace, choose to stay lost. Linger and loiter in such lavish and gifted serenity of soul.

Soul Questions to Slow Your Stride

- What is the crux of the disturbance within?
- How do I benefit from always being on the go?
- Why do I feel threatened?
- What do I fear losing?
- What do I fear gaining?
- How does it make me feel to stop running?
- Who will I be if I stop running?

A Power Letter from God

Dear Sacred One,

As my beloved child, you are both product and recipient of My creative energy. Each day, you are called to be about the business of owning a little more of your power. Learn to enjoy embracing the aliveness that enlivens, abiding in you. The best way to fully realize your human strength is to be firmly convinced of the divine strength within you. Don't be afraid to claim all that is in you to claim. Do this and your possibility will always loom larger than your challenge.

Eternally and Internally Yours,
Your Loving Creator

Linger Awhile

Notice
when and where
your soul
wants you
to linger awhile.

Soul Thirst

To know

what your soul

is thirsty for

is to know

God's dream

for you.

Just Feel Peace

Often,

all your soul

will want

for you

is to just

let yourself

feel peace.

Soul Ovation

Your soul

will still

be clapping

in all out

approval

of you

when all others

have stopped.

Down is Not Done

To

be

down

is

not

to

be

done.

5

Be Honest

Where Your Secrets are Safe

There is a compliment my wife pays me that makes me feel great and humbly proud every time she repeats it. Usually it is said in response to someone sharing a personal matter with her that they are surprised she knows absolutely nothing about. They assume that she knows thinking I had shared the matter with them. My wife will say, "My husband never does that. If you tell him something in confidence, he won't tell anyone, not even me." As good as my record on confidentiality may be, I am not the best at it, your soul is. When it comes to hearing and holding, your soul will never let you down. Your soul is a place where your secrets are safe.

One of the magnificent benefits of soul talk is that it affords you a preeminent dialogical partner you can share anything at all with, without fear that what you have shared will be shared. There is always a place we can go with our deepest secrets. And such space is vital to our mental, emotional, and spiritual health. What we fail to own up to may end up owning us in unflattering and unhealthy ways. Get in the habit of being as honest as you can with your soul. Your wholeness, wellness, and growth is your soul's agenda.

Take advantage of your inner chamber of confession and celebration. That's right celebration. The soul is not only a place to express our innermost challenges, but also feelings of happiness over events, experiences and revelations. Claiming your mountaintops is as vital as owning your valleys. Don't be ashamed of your joy.

Your Feelings and Being Fully Human

All of your feelings matter, even the ones you would not want anyone to know about. Spirituality that does not honor the full spectrum of human expression is not in our best interests. One of the things I find most fascinating about Jesus is his fabulous full humanness. Not only was he unafraid of dying, but just as importantly, he was unafraid of being fully alive, and living again. Living for Jesus meant feeling joy and pain, and everything in between. He was so in touch with his feelings that at least once he freely cried in public, at the tomb of Lazarus. Notably, God did not make Jesus stop crying.

Our tears matter.

Our anger matters. Being fully human includes learning to trust your strong emotion, including being extremely mad. How much permission do you give yourself to be deeply upset? The goal ought not be to avoid deep anger at all cost, but to learn to direct feelings of deep anger toward consideration and growth. Soul talk conversation is a safe space to own your rage, helping to insure that such anger does not evolve into entrenched resentment, possibly leading to destructive violent behavior. Through the gentle and sustained guidance of your soul, you will be inspired to grace yourself as you are, and use the transformative energy generated by grace to keep on keeping on.

We do not do God or ourselves any favors by denying the holy gift of our honest feelings. Our feelings help us to savor life. Our feelings help us to more deeply and genuinely connect with each other. Our feelings help us to be in touch with our deeper selves. Without knowing our feelings, we cannot know who we really are, and who we really want to be. Honesty about our feelings helps us to feel whole when life starts falling apart.

The Spiritual Gold of Desire

A part of hearing our feelings out in soul talk is hearing our desires out. Too often when we speak of desire, our reference is to burning passion for physical intimacy. As holy a gift as that is, desire is much bigger than that, and so is passion. The truth of the matter is, God speaks to us through all of our wholesome desires and passions. One of the most effective ways to uncover God's will for your life is to excavate during your soul talks what you effortlessly love. What makes you come alive was placed there by God.

Honesty about Suffering

My friend and colleague in pastoral ministry, Rev. Rose Wright-Scott, has written a marvelous book about overcoming layered adversity. One of the potent strengths of *Finding Sanity in the Stress,* is its relentless honesty:

> *I am a godly person. Surely this thing is about to move, because I've declared, decreed, and told the devil, he's a liar. I smile. I suffer in silence because everyone keeps telling me how strong I am, but if only they knew. I know this may seem anti-faith but it is my choice to be transparent. Quoting scriptures, and rebuking devils did not bring me sanity nor peace in the middle of the stress. As much as I served un-selfishly, and gave so generously to others, it was not enough. No, it took: Admitting that I was human, and that it was ok to be; Acknowledging that I did not always have the answers and that it was ok not to....*

Pastor Scott's testimony is refreshing. Genuine strength is honest about heartache.

In his classic, *Care of the Soul,* Thomas Moore teaches a delicate lesson about honesty with suffering:

> *Care of the soul... appreciates the mystery of hu-man suffering and does not offer the illusion of a problem-free life. It sees every fall into ignorance*

and confusion as an opportunity to discover that the beast residing at the center of the labyrinth is also an angel.

The soul knows the reality of suffering, and will not deny it. The soul knows that break-throughs are sometimes held up, and that deliverance is often delayed. In such moments, wholeness can feel hollow. Yet, it is not just our "together" that is blessed by God, but our "un-together." We need not wait to see the silver lining in the cloud to feel graced. Dark clouds are no less heavenly. In the mystery of grace, being honest about our suffering and sorrow can somehow be redemptive.

You Have to Face It to Fix It

I had never felt such hurt before. I had been blindsided by someone I deeply respected and never saw it coming. The moment was bad enough, but I kept replaying it over and over in my mind making matters worse. How could he? What was he thinking? Why didn't I see this coming? Along with the hurt from the wrong inflicted by someone I admired was the ensuing guilt for feeling sustained anger and rage against this person. This lasted for sometime.

What I learned was unexpressed bitterness festers, becoming a force of self-diminishment. My healing came when I began to be honest with my soul about how I was feeling. My soul didn't judge me; my soul heard me out. Eventually, I was able to confess my feelings to the offender, and there was a restoration of respect. It did not happen overnight. Many wounds are slow to heal. And some memories take a long time to stop hurting, if they ever do. Yet, there is something that your soul will remind you of over and over again: *No matter how deep the hurt, God's love is deeper. And just because you're still hurting doesn't mean the healing hasn't started.*

Whatever feels broken inside, you have to face it to fix it. Soul talk time is as good a time as any to put it all on the table, using words that tell the truth about your wounds. Your healing is only as deep as your willingness to confess the depth of your pain. Tell the truth to your soul about how much you are hurting.

Honest Opposition to Soul

What happens when our soul offers guidance that we reject? All we need do is be honest about the objection. The truth is the truth is the truth. It does no good for us to pretend we are in a place where we are not. Better to confess our unwillingness to heed the soul's call than to be indifferent or completely numb to it.

You will discover that your soul does not find your resistance unacceptable. Resistance is something that the soul knows how to work with through grace, mercy, and patient persistence. Your soul is effortlessly cool in this way. Your soul knows how to wait you out. It will wait until you are ready to receive. When your soul ceases petitioning you on something that truly matters, your soul is merely pausing; it is not giving up.

Honesty Hunt Questions

- How do I really feel?

- What do I feel good about?

- What is troubling me?

- What do I really want?

- What am I afraid of?

Show Yourself

Honesty

makes it

possible

for the

real you

to show

up in life.

Being true

to yourself

begins with

being true

to your soul.

Risky Honesty

Beyond

risky honesty

is living freedom

too wonderful

to miss.

Your Courageous Soul

Be encouraged

by your soul;

for your soul

knows too much

to ever be afraid.

Necessary Cease-Fire

Cease

warring against

what has already

been decided

in your soul.

6

Be Gentle

The Power of a Gentle Touch

In **November, 2017,** I was diagnosed with Type 2 diabetes. During my hospitalization, something happened that moved me deeply. I was resting when I felt a hand brush lightly and slowly across my forehead, first one way, and then the other. The hand then slid down both sides of my face. Amid the touching, came forth these words of greeting, "Oh, Man of God." As I opened my eyes, I saw a face I had never seen before. It turned out to be one of my physicians.

Manfred Ernesti's reputation had preceded him. Another doctor had told me he would be stopping by, and that the 87-year-old healer was much beloved by staff and patients for his wisdom and way. For the next forty minutes or so, I sat enthralled by this enchanted healer-sage. We spoke of my condition, and so much more, including the recent death of his beloved wife. He had held her hand as she passed away. In his own words, "I knew the exact moment when she was gone." I did not doubt it because I knew there was something special about his touch based on the way he had touched me a moment ago.

While I have forgotten some of the things Dr. Ernesti shared with me on that day, I have never forgotten his gentle touch. We never know how much such a touch can mean until it is rendered and noticed. As you engage your soul talk sessions, pay attention to your soul's gentle touch. May you be as gentle with yourself as your soul is with you.

Going in Grace

How Jesus came back to life matters almost as much as the fact *that* he did. When Jesus came back to life, he took his time to lovingly greet Mary, casually walk with two persons who thought he was a stranger on the Emmaus Road, gracefully address Thomas's doubts, and gently encourage and reassure Peter. There is excitement in his return, but no hurry or strain. His resurrection is dripping with grace, lavish unconditional esteem and acceptance, as much as it is with glorious challenging new possibility.

The extravagant grace with which Jesus lived his new life is a model for how we may live ours. In a culture characterized by stressing, pushing, and proving, how wonderful is it to know that new life, as portrayed by Jesus, is much more about grace than it is about going, going, and going until you drop.

Jesus says in Matthew 11:28-29:

> *Come to me, all you that are carrying heavy burdens,*
> *and I will give you rest. Take my yoke upon you and*
> *learn from me, for I am gentle and humble in heart,*
> *and you will find rest in your souls.*

Ease of soul is God's desire for you. This desire will shine forth in your soul's approach and conversation. If things ever get too tense in your soul talk, the source is never your soul. Grace is your soul's calling card.

Receiving God's Un-Provoked Grace

In John 12:1-8, Jesus is eating with his disciples and receiving the lavish anointing of Mary. Judas, under the guise of missionary concern, attempts to end Mary's generous show of affection. Jesus will have none of it. He tells Judas, in essence, to shut up and mind his own business. The role reversal of Jesus as recipient as opposed to giver is significant, and so is the pictorial image. Not only does Jesus accept the role of the receiver, but he reclines into the role, savors it, and resists all attempts to snatch it from him. Jesus seems as used to receiving as he is to giving.

Your soul talk moments will have you on the receiving end of challenge and conviction, but also magnificent peace and joy. While we grow up being taught to ask for God's blessings, often fully receiving God's blessings takes some getting used to. Learning to receive God's blessings is one of the sweet challenges of life. Regarding this, your soul has a secret to share: *There is no need to provoke God to bless. God's posture to bless precedes your desire to be blessed.*

How good can you become at receiving God's unprovoked grace day in and day out, moment by moment, step by step?

We All Need God's Grace to Stand

In his book, *The Yellow Leaves*, Frederick Buechner remembers seeing President Franklin Roosevelt, who had been crippled by polio, in a hotel elevator:

> *Even all these years later I can still remember the moment when the double doors of the elevator rumbled softly apart and there was Franklin D. Roosevelt framed in the wide opening. He was standing between two men, taller of whom, my mother whispered, was one of his sons. Each of them had hold of him under one of his arms, and I could see that if they let him go, he would crumble to the ground....*
>
> *What I learned for the first time from the glimpse I had of him in the elevator is that even the mightiest among us can't stand on our own.*

We all need God's grace to stand. When such grace is offered in your soul talks, take it. Take it again, again, and again.

Your Soul's Beautiful Bunting

In baseball, a beautifully placed bunt to advance runners can be as important as a home run. To bunt well, one needs to have the strength of gentleness. Expert bunters know how to allow ball to touch bat in precise and particular ways. Force gives way to finesse. Bunting hinges on a batter's gentle touch. Bunting is baseball at its gentle best. A beautifully executed bunt is a beautiful thing to behold.

Your soul will not shy away from showing you places in yourself where you can be and do better. But, it will always do so with a gentle touch. Notice when your soul bunts. When your soul raises a concern that you may have forgotten about that warrants more attention. It may be about something said to someone that was taken the wrong way. We may unintentionally wound with words and deeds without even noticing. The soul may bunt by way of an awareness of a matter you may have settled in your mind but not your heart. The soul's bunt may be one of conviction, not to weigh you down, but to help you live with a lighter load. Remember when your soul bunts to be as gentle with yourself as your soul was with its delicate hand in drawing your attention.

A Love Letter from God

Dear Child,

I love you for you. Let go and let yourself feel loved. All the love you deserve and thought you never had is yours right now, But you must let me love you. All the sunshine in the world means nothing if you won't see the light or feel the warmth. Let me love you, and then live my love.

Love You Madly,
God

Lovely Soul Truth

Believe it when your soul says,

"The great delusion is that

you have to earn your worthiness.

You are God's gift before you

offer up anything at all."

Grace Catch

There

is

no

fall

that

grace

can't

catch.

Special Delivery

After giving your all

to so much

and so many,

take some time now

to deliver yourself

to your soul

and rest awhile.

Light Sufficient

When you can't see
the whole way through,
trust the light you have.

You Too

Take it easy
on yourself.
Grace is for
you too.

I Feel Good!

Let
yourself
feel
good
about
feeling
good.

What God Whispered

What if

at the

conclusion of

singing

"How Great

Thou Art,"

you heard

God whisper,

"You too"?

7

Welcome New Truth

God is Always Thinking Greater Than The Blessing You Have in Mind

When hard pressed, I cried to the Lord; He brought me into a spacious place.

Psalm 118:5

Lucille Clifton suggests that in order to do it well, you must be willing to move "from here to there," all the while, "blessing the boats" that grant us safe, if at at times, upsetting passage. Duke Ellington believed that he was doing it best when his ears were "10 feet high." Howard Thurman said it hinged on our intentionally focusing on "the growing edge." Ellen Langer believes that the critical keys to its realization are continuous creation of new categories, openness to new information, and awareness of multiple perspectives. Jesus said, "You must be born again."

The references are to being changed over and over again, to being in the words of another, "continual changing changeful selves." Such is not possible without intentionally welcoming new truth. Your soul wishes to assist you in this process, not only delivering transformation but helping you to dance it as well.

Sometimes we all can be very stubborn, especially when it comes to holding on to something that once gave us what we once needed. Perhaps the most difficult growth of all is when we feel ourselves drifting away from that which once drew us. And yet such separation must occur if we are to evolve into our fullest expressions of ourselves.

Our soul voice assists us in such necessary growth by offering and repeating growth guidance. Notice when your soul insists. Pay careful attention to repeated messages, to guidance you may hear expressed differently but which carries the same certain message. Hearing and heeding such guidance can offer sweet relief sufficient enough to rival the sometimes necessary pain of transformation.

Make Space For Your New Self

Into the Magic Shop: A Neurosurgeon's Quest to Discover the Mysteries of the Brain and Secrets of the Heart, includes the following testimony by author James R. Doty:

What I do know for sure is that I have died many times in this life. As a lost and hopeless boy, I died in a magic shop. The young man who was both ashamed and terrified of his father, the one who had struck him and got his blood on his hands, died the day he went off to college. And although I didn't know it at the time of my accident, eventually the arrogant, egotistical neurosurgeon I would become would also suffer his own death. We can die a thousand times in this lifetime, and that is one of the gifts of being alive.

Doty's identifying transformation with death is noteworthy. It suggests that growth may be impaired by an unwillingnesses to give up the body and ghost of an old self. On the other hand, transformation may be enhanced by a willingness to not just tolerate change, but to take steps to urge on transformation in a spirit of celebration and anticipation. When your soul teases you with a vision of a new version of yourself, behold the new image. And when the time comes and the courage becomes sufficient, let it live. When Jesus says, "You must be born again," you have to think he has more in mind than your just being a new version of your old self.

Grab Hold to What Your Soul Holds

As you become more sensitive to your inner voice, you will become more attentive to what matters most, because your soul always knows what matters most. Thus, you may find yourself suddenly paying surprise deep attention to something that you may have not noticed initially. For example, earlier this year after viewing the movie, *Black Panther*, I left the theater impressed, but not as overwhelmed as I was prepared to be given the movie's pre-showing buzz. But the next morning, I discovered that my mind was ablaze with scenes and themes from the movie. I began writing on one of the several small notepads I have scattered around our home. My notes turned into this social media post:

> *The Delightful and Liberating Gospel According to Black Panther:*
>
> *You have a divine right to choose your own path.*
>
> *Heritage must not only be revered, but responsibly explored and challenged.*
>
> *Salvation outside an ever-widening sense of community is a selfish delusion.*
>
> *Genuine power is as playfully creative as it is potently fierce.*

Though I don't remember reflecting much on this extraordinary movie immediately after viewing it, apparently my soul ruminated on it all night long as I slept, to the point that when I arose the next morning, the movie's meaning was all I could think about without trying to think about it at all. Attend to what your soul grabs hold of and will not let go.

Living in Freedom Flow

The term "freedom flow" came to mind one afternoon as I sought to name the lessened strain and stress I was feeling about life in general, and my preaching, teaching, and writing labor in particular. I felt that perhaps some of the weightlessness was due to intentional steps taken to lighten my load. Also, I attributed the palpable new ease to years of experience that permits certain assurances one does not have when starting out. And yet, I felt something more was at work, beyond less labor and experiencing the fringe benefits of professional experience.

I wrote the following words: "less weighed down by desire to prove this or that or do this or that. Living feels lighter. In freedom flow mode, being and doing are lighter. Freedom flow facilitates a more relaxed attitude toward and engagement with life." If you asked me to be more definitive about freedom flow, I would say the following.

Freedom flow is a living expression characterized by soul ease, lightheartedness, and peaceful excitement. In freedom flow, one feels less weighed down by internal and external expectation and obligation. Being and doing are influenced by an abiding deeply relaxed spirit, daringly and delightfully open to what is.

So what does freedom flow have to do soul talk? I suspect that listening to my soul more regularly, is, in part, responsible for my freedom flow. My soul is the freest part of my being. Moreover, its natural beat is in keeping with the divine rhythm beneath all that was, is, and will be. Why wouldn't a deeper awareness and accessing of my soul result in a palpable living experience characterized by less stress and strain and more peace and effortless empowerment?

God is Always and Forever Dreaming Your Joy

New truth that may jar us initially, always has joy for a purpose. We are the result of God dreaming our joy. That soul pleasure is an ultimate purpose for living is not hedonistic; it is holy.

One of the magnificent features of the purest joy is that it is transcendent. Pure joy, a lavish sense of it being well with your soul, does not need optimal circumstances to exist. The purest joy is a strangely undeniable sense of fullness of spirit. And it can be present in the most threatening circumstances. One striking example of it is the palpable vibrancy of Martin Luther King, Jr. evident during his "I've Been to the Mountaintop" sermon delivered on the eve of his death. Though he speaks of social horrors and personal hurts, the spirit of the sermon is one of euphoric hope and promise. The purest joy remains joy in the storms and valleys of life.

Return, Remember, and Journey On

One night I had a two vivid dreams. The first had me returning to a time when I was a boy preacher in New Orleans, Louisiana. I remember greeting persons who were some of my early supporters. I felt their loving embraces and pride. The second dream had me traveling up a steep mountain. The vehicle moved at a steady and safe pace, and it needed to. I was traveling a mountain road going higher and higher, with no railing on the opposite side of the mountain. One false jerk and I would be into the mountain or free fall. That having been said, there was a peace about the movement onward and upward. I awakened wanting to understand the connections between both dreams if there were any. I did not have to ponder long for what seemed to be the lesson that was intended to stick: Returning and remembering are best experienced in service to our onward journey.

To be inspired by our past is one thing; to be enslaved by our past is another. To be enslaved to our past is to frustrate the ongoing flow of life. When we return to the past and feel loving reassurance, we may be empowered to engage new adventures and explorations. What we hold dear should never be allowed to hold us back.

As you grow, seek to discover new things about yourself that may surprise and even disturb you. Dare to be you in all your diverse and widening wonder. Resist needing your many sides to blend or be complimentary. God's splendid grace secures your manifold splendor.

Hosting New Truth Questions

What do you love most?
What do you really want most of all?
What won't you drop?
What are your deepest desires?
What feels magical to you?

What helps to open up your life?
What holds you bound?
What do you hold the keys to?
How are you moving forward in your life?

What new risks have you taken?
What are you most curious about?
What new adventures and challenges are you engaging?
What do you feel dying within you?

What do you feel coming alive within you?
Where do you see the face of God?

Soul Talk Affirmations

An effective way of utilizing soul talk guidance to altar your mind-set and behavior on behalf of your scared transformation is to turn soul wisdom into affirmations, statements of beliefs that are easily repeatable. Positive living affirmations charge and recharge us with vital living energy, purpose, and direction. Best used, affirmations keep us on track with what is true. Here are some of my favorite Soul Talk Affirmations:

> *I see myself entering a new season of grace for ful-filling my sacred desires.*
>
> *My peace is inexhaustible and portable.*
>
> *What is in me is greater than what is against me.*
>
> *I aspire from a place of deep contentment.*
>
> *I go in grace, step in peace, and walk in love.*
>
> *I join others in creating the beloved community.*
>
> *It is well with my soul.*

I encourage you to draft, repeat, and internalize your personal Soul Talk Affirmations. If you don't mind doing so, please share them with me at kjones58@aol.com.

What Makes God Smile?

God smiles

when you

are smitten

by what

soulfully

enchants you.

New Flame Burning

A passion

need not

be eternal.

Sometimes

you have to let

an old fire go out

for a new flame

to burn bright.

Soul Says Move On

Stop feeding
with desire
what means you
no good.

Move on.

Some doors
need to be closed
and never
opened again.

Move on.

You can't
go on
and hold on
at the same time.

Move on.
Move on.
Move on.

Permission Granted

Take a moment
to grant permission
for a new possibility
to rise up inside you.

Epilogue

Claiming Soul Talk Blessings for Everyday Life

In-Visioning is one of my morning rituals. For about ten minutes or so, I see in my spirit, sense in my heart, and settle in my soul something I wish to realize in my life during the day. On some days, I know what I wish to in-vision before beginning the process. On other days, I wait for the subject to surface. One day, what surfaced surprised and enchanted me. What I I desired to manifest not just in my life that day but continually, was a sense of living ease that had me naturally comfortable with less hurry and a lighter load. Where had such a desire come from? I believe it come from my soul talks.

Soul talks tend to be characterized by patience, spaciousness, lightheartedness, and graciousness. The soul is never in a hurry to say or to have you understand. Moreover, there is an ever-present spaciousness for hearing and hearing again. Your soul is the most hospitable place in the world. Even when the subject matter is serious, the soul has a way of communicating with a light and affirming touch. Indeed, the heavier the subject, the lighter the touch. Soul atmosphere, never put upon, by an overly judgmental mindset, is one of graceful acceptance, affirmation, and understanding.

What I In-Visioned that day was for the peaceful climate of my soul talk to find its way into the natural ebb and flow of my every day life. I wanted my soul talk atmosphere to inform my attitudes, actions, and pace in my life for the rest of my life.

The more time you spend in soul talk sessions, the more you will become accustomed to what peace, margin, and a bearable load feel like. You will grow to love and long for that feeling. Loving and longing will lead you to do what you need to do to allow the fresh breeze of soul talk to blow freely in your life, for the gracious good of all.

Honor Your Soul Talk with Your Bold Walk

One of the great tragedies of life is ignoring soul guidance once it has come. To hear soul speak is not the end of our responsibility to the soul. Even when soul speak is comforting, we are challenged to own the peace of mind being offered to us. With enhanced soul talk comes a greater responsibility to act on what we hear, lest our soul's guidance be in vein. To take more responsibility for living the soul's leading, reflect regularly by journaling, and going back to read what you have written. This will allow you to identify and trace your growth steps. Along with journaling, share some of your soul's leading with a trusted friend and grant them permission to help you remain faithful to your growth. To hear the soul speak is one thing, to heed the soul's guidance is something else all together. Prayers that replace responsibility need not be prayed. Being open to the Spirit does not diminish deliberate and creative engagement with life. Genuine praying to God inspires active playing with God.

Go Bold; Don't Hold Back!

Early one morning last December, I had just finished meditating on my goals for the new year approaching, when I heard a loud buzzing noise. A fly had come to listen in. Initially annoyed, I quickly did something that has become a habit: I looked up the symbolism of the animal that had made a sudden appearance in my life. I learned that the fly "serves as a reminder that you reap what you sow," and that it "symbolized abundance and prosperity during times of adversity." This sentence really grabbed me: "It sends the message that being persistent, consistent, and determined even in the face of tragedy will result to victory." Needless to say, that fly lived to see another day.

I imagined that the fly, rather than coming to annoy me, had, in enchanting fact, appeared to encourage me. A mantra that I had already embraced received a hearty amen from my small but mighty visitor: Go Bold; Don't Hold Back!

As you cultivate your soul dialogue habit, join it with the habit of honoring your soul talk with your bold walk. Go Bold; Don't Hold Back! Going Bold is imagining and living your grandest dreams. Going Bold is being consistent, persistent, and determined, through it all and come what may. Going Bold is achieving what you set out to achieve or better, No Holding Back!

Something Within You

In his wonderful autobiography, *Treat it Gentle,* legendary jazz clarinetist, Sidney Bechet, makes the following observation about the difference between bands that played just what they knew and bands that played what they knew and more:

You know, when you learn something, you can go just so far. When you've finished that, there's not much else you can do unless you know how to get hold of something inside you that isn't learned. It has to be there inside you without any need of learning. The band that played what it knew, it didn't have enough. In the end it would get confused; it was finished. And the people, they could tell.

The phrase "get hold of something inside you" captivates me. It reminds me of words Jesus kept saying over and over again to people: "The Kingdom of God is within you." You have something within that speaks life to death, up to down, faith to failure, healing to hurt, hope to despair, and joy to sorrow. Your soul will never ever let you forget this good news.

Soul Talk and Choosing New Life

I am concluding this manuscript during the magnificent season of Resurrection. The Spirit of New Life is in the air. Yet though such a Spirit is loose in the world, it is possible to live oblivious to it. We can choose to ignore inspiration. Even Jesus, the Risen One, may have done so.

What if after the stone was rolled away from the tomb, Jesus refused to come out? Upon being resurrected, Jesus might have opted to remain in the tomb. He who was raised had to choose to make his exit from the tomb. Divine inspiration always awaits our response.

New life may be held up inside a tomb. As you feel your spiritual lungs filling with the restorative breath of vibrant new life, let nothing keep you from coming out, from reengaging life with fresh energy and excitement. The Spirit does not raise you to stay in the tomb. The Spirit does not raise you to stay hidden in fear, shame, guilt, and regret. As you come into your fullest, freshest, and finest self, let nothing keep you from coming out. Choose to respond to divine inspiration with human initiative and resolve.

Once risen, don't be afraid to step out. Jesus did not get up for you to stay down.

Your soul will continually encourage you to embrace divine inspiration with human initiative. Soul talk ought never be seen as a denial of or replacement for human responsibility-taking. Dynamic faithful existence is divine inspiration dancing with human initiative. To pray and never take a step or make a move is to leave God standing alone on the dance floor. God told Moses, as God tells us to, "Be still," but God never says, "Be still forever." Once guided by your soul's divine wisdom, don't be afraid to make your move. The movement within to converse with your soul should inspire you to make your move, to move out, and to move on! Soul talk always serves new resolve, new action, and new life. There is no limit to what God can do through a person risen anew with an open, willing, and trusting heart. Urged ever onward by your gentle and gallant soul, stand up strong in your growing wisdom, experience, and power!

Unstoppable Soul Song and Dance

In a wonderful video, a passenger is riding along in the front seat of a vehicle when a favorite song comes on. It was, I learned, a gospel song by Alicia Meyers, "I Wanna Thank You," remixed to a really catchy soulful rhythmic beat. The passenger begins moving in her seat until she can no longer remain seated. In an infectious display of spontaneous delight, she demands that the driver let her out of the car, "Let me out! Let me out of the car! Let me out right now!" Once out, she begins to sing and dance freely from street to sidewalk. She is singing and dancing from the depths of her soul, where her singing and dancing began. You don't have to be a songwriter for your soul to give you a song, and a reason to sing and dance.

Soul Delight

May you

notice

when your

soul sings,

dances,

and shouts,

"Yes!"

Soul Benediction

Go in Grace.

Step in Peace.

Walk in Love.

Just Trust that God is with You,

And You Will Always Have

Just the Strength

You Need.

"Your Soul is your
hidden reservoir of limitless
wisdom, peace, and joy."

7 Soul Talk Steps

1. Be Still.
2. Lay Burdens Down.
3. Listen Deeply.
4. Don't Run Away.
5. Be Honest.
6. Be Gentle.
7. Welcome New Truth.

50 Personal And Group Discussion Questions

Chapter One Be Still

How many biblical references to stillness can you recall?

How do you define stillness?

What makes stillness hard to achieve?

What are your favorite ways of being still?

How has/does stillness bless your life?

What can you do to become better at at stillness?

How can stillness become more integral to your private devotion and public worship?

How can we help each other to practice stillness?

Chapter Two Lay Burdens Down

What heavy burdens are you presently carrying?

How many biblical references to peace of soul can you identify?

How do you relieve stress?

What is the difference between physical and soul stress?
How can stress prohibit deeper attention to your soul?
How does peace of mind assist soul communication?

Chapter Three Listen Deeply

How would you rate yourself as a listener?
What is the difference between listening and listening deeply?
Can you identify several instances in which Jesus excelled as a listener?
Who would you identify as a great listener?
What supports listening deeply?
What prevents listening deeply?
What are the rewards of listening deeply to ourselves and others?

Chapter Four Don't Run Away

Why do we run?
How do you define fear?
How do you define courage?
Can fear and courage exist together?
What specific steps can you take to resist running away?
Are there times when running away is necessary?

Chapter Five Be Honest

How do you define honesty?
When has honesty helped you?
How has honesty hurt you?

What are the benefits of honesty?

How does honesty help us to grow?

How can we encourage honesty in communication and friendship?

Chapter Six Be Gentle

How do you define gentleness?

Where do you see gentleness modeled in Scripture?

Who are the gentle souls in your life?

Can you identify a situation where gentleness made all the difference in the world?

Why is it important to be gentle with ourselves?

What is the relationship between gentleness and patience?

Chapter Seven Welcome New Truth

What are some biblical references to transformation?

How may we resist change?

How can we become more deeply curious?

How might curiosity melt fear?

How can we support transformation in each other?

What is your response to the following:

"Your soul has a knack for teasing and taunting you with new spaces of possibility."?

What specific messages are you presently receiving from your soul urging you onward and upward?

General Questions

How has the book *Soul Talk* helped you most?

What *Soul Talk* steps do you find easiest?

What *Soul Talk* step do you find hardest?

How do you suggest making soul talk sessions more fun?

What Your Soul Says Is Worth Remembering

NOW AVAILABLE AT AMAZON.COM

Soul Talk Coaching Sessions

Your *Soul Talk* has the power to change your life for the best. You owe it to your life to do all you can to initiate and sustain that change.

Soul Talk Coaching Sessions with long-time pastor, professor, and author, Kirk Byron Jones, D.Min., Ph.D., are designed to help you:

- Attain greater insight and skill regarding the 7 Soul Talk steps.

- Become better able to discern your soul's unique voice.

- Apply Soul Talk guidance to personal and professional decision-making.

- Cultivate new living confidence to match your new soul clarity.

- Increase your capacity for holding challenging and uncomfortable truth.

- Learn empowering journaling strategies and practices.

- Receive guidance for your personal questions and challenges, and more.

To schedule or learn more about **Soul Talk Coaching Sessions**, contact Kirk Byron Jones at Kjones58@aol.com or call 781-963-3276.

A Personal Request

Thank you for your time and attention. I hope *Soul Talk* has blessed you in marvelous ways, including ways beyond my dreams and intentions. If this has been the case, I ask you to share a brief testimony/review of how *Soul Talk* has benefited you at amazon.com. Your words, no matter how brief, will help spread the *Soul Talk* message in the world.

I am also interested in any responses or questions you may have regarding *Soul Talk*. I would very much appreciate hearing about your experiences with *SoulTalk*. Please contact me at kjones58@aol.com. I genuinely look forward to your sharing.

Yours in Wild and Wonderful Soul Talk Adventure,
Kirk Byron Jones
April, 2018

About Kirk Byron Jones

Born in New Orleans, Louisiana, as the second son to the late Frederick and Ora Mae Jones, Kirk Byron Jones is a graduate of Loyola University and Andover Newton Theological School, and holds a Doctor of Ministry degree from Emory University and a Doctor of Philosophy degree from Drew University.

Dr. Jones began preaching at age 12, and has served as a pastor for over thirty years. He was the founding minister of Beacon Light Baptist Church in New Orleans, and Senior Minister at Calvary Baptist Church, Chester, PA; Ebenezer Baptist Church, Boston, MA; and the First Baptist Churches of Randolph and Tewksbury MA. He presently serves as Senior Pastor of Zion Baptist Church in Lynn, Massachusetts. Throughout his pastoral ministry, Rev. Jones has served on various religious and civic committees at the local and national level.

A professor for over twenty-five years, Dr. Jones has served as Director of the Kelsey-Owens Black Ministries Program and Kelsey-Owens Professor at Andover Newton Theological School. Currently an adjunct professor of social ethics, preaching, and pastoral ministry at Andover Newton Theological School, Dr. Jones serves as guest preacher and teacher at churches, schools and conferences throughout the United States. His writings have been published in various journals, including The Christian Century, Leadership, Gospel Today, Pulpit Digest, and The African American Pulpit, a quarterly preaching journal he co-founded in 1997.

Dr. Jones is the author of many books for clergy, and all persons seeking spiritual growth in a changing and challenging world. His books include the following titles:

- *Rest in the Storm: Self-Care Strategies for Clergy and Other Caregivers*

- *Addicted to Hurry: Spiritual Strategies for Slowing Down*

- *The Jazz of Preaching: How to Preach with Great Freedom and Joy*

- *Morning B.R.E.W.: A Divine Power Drink for Your Soul*

- *Holy Play: The Joyful Adventure of Unleashing Your Divine Purpose*

- *Fulfilled: Living and Leading with Unusual Wisdom, Peace, and Joy*

- *Just Because You're in a Storm Doesn't Mean the Storm has to be in You*

Dr. Jones is the creator/author of the Facebook page "Yes to Grace" where he offers brief inspirational messages in words and images. Currently, "Yes to Grace" has nearly 200,000 subscribers. For more information about his writing and teaching ministry, you may visit www.kirkbjones.com.

Dr. Jones is married to Mary Brown-Jones. They have 4 adult children, 3 grandchildren, and reside in Randolph, MA. When not engaged in the holy play of his labor, he enjoys leisurely fun, most especially: reading, journaling, listening to and learning about jazz, playing video games, and beholding sunsets.

Made in the USA
Columbia, SC
10 November 2018